Made Simple

TOOL
SHARPENING

John Perkins

150mm (6")
BENCH GRINDER
MODEL No. BG150CX

MOTOR:	
AMPS:	1/2HP (370W)
VOLTAGE:	1.7A
SPEED:	240V 1ph 50Hz
AXLE:	3000 RPM
WHEEL:	13mm (1/2")
	150mm x 20mm x 13mm
	6" x 3/4 - 2 1/2"

DATE: U.K. DISTRIBUTOR,
NATIONAL MACHINERY, BURY ST. EDMUNDS, SUFFOLK

OFF
0

ON
I

Made Simple

TOOL
SHARPENING

John Perkins

Bloomsbury Books
London

Made Simple
TOOL SHARPENING

Page 2:   A dry stone bench grinder with gouges and a scraper (see page 42).

This edition published in 1994 by Bloomsbury Books,

an imprint of   The Godfrey Cave Group,
42 Bloomsbury Street, London. WC1B 3QJ

Under license from   Harlaxton Publishing Limited
2 Avenue Road, Grantham, Lincolnshire, NG31 6TA, United Kingdom.
A member of the Weldon International Group of Companies.

Publisher: Robin Burgess
Design and Coordination: Rachel Rush
Editing: Martyn Hocking
Illustrator: David Cook, Linden Artists
Photography: Chris Allen, Forum Advertising Limited
Typesetting: Seller's, Grantham
Colour Reproduction: GA Graphics, Stamford
Printing: Imago, Singapore

British Library Cataloguing-in-Publication data.
A catalogue record for this book is available from the British Library.
Title: Made Simple - TOOL SHARPENING
ISBN: 1-85471-382-5

Made Simple

CONTENTS

A ll cutting tools, whether they are used for woodworking, gardening, hobbies or in the kitchen, need to be kept in good condition and – above everything else – sharp.

A blunt knife will make a mess of carving the Sunday joint just as surely as a blunt saw will spoil your effort to cut a professional-looking woodworking joint.

While you might consider throwing away a cheap tool when it loses its edge – and these days, some budget-priced saws are made of materials that are actually impossible to re-sharpen – quality products should give a lifetime of service if you look after them.

Sharpening is an art that has been wrapped up in a fair bit of mystery by professionals over the years, but the truth is that anyone can learn to look after their own tools.

Some basic sharpening equipment will need to be bought, but this will pay for itself many times over by extending the life of your tools and improving the quality of the work you can accomplish with them.

OPPOSITE: A purpose built tool bench in a converted and dedicated workshop.

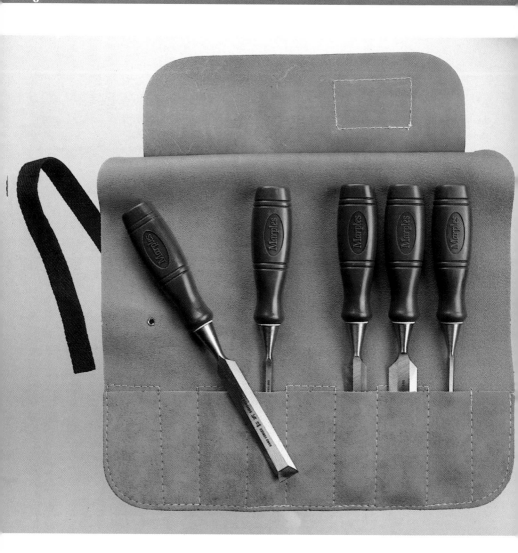

ABOVE: A simple yet practical leather roll for storing chisels safely.

Tools become blunt through repeated use, but we are all guilty of accelerating this process by storing and carrying them in a careless way.

No cutting edge can be expected to stay sharp if it is continually knocking against other tools. Likewise a layer of rust and the 'pitting' this leaves behind on the surface of the metal when the rust has been cleaned off will create extra friction and prevent the blade from slicing easily through the work.

To prevent this type of damage, it is important to store your tools carefully, both in the workshop and when in transit.

How you store them will depend very much on how and where you use them. If most of your work is done in a home workshop, garden shed or garage, you may prefer to keep them in racks or open storage where they will be readily to hand. If you use them primarily for repair work around the home, you will want to be able to carry them with you.

TOOL STORAGE

Unless your workshop is heated and kept at a reasonably constant temperature, leaving your tools in the open can be detrimental to their long-term health.

Fluctuating temperature and humidity levels will quickly lead to rust formation. This is a particular problem where tools are not being used regularly, as the basic cutting action will generally remove any fine surface rusting before it goes any deeper.

Another cause of partial rusting is the sweat that forms on your hands as you work. You may notice this in particular at the top of chisel blades or where your forefinger rests on the top of a plane-iron. Sap from unseasoned wood can also cause rust to start to form.

PREVENTING RUST

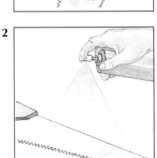

W̲henever you finish using your tools for the day, there are things you can do to protect them against rust.

1 Wipe them over with a dry cloth before smearing the bare parts with a thin coat of machine oil. This is a very effective way to keep rust at bay, but it can be slightly messy and time-consuming, and the oil will need to be removed from the tools before working with them again, to avoid marring the surface of the wood. Oil can also prevent some wood finishes adhering properly or cause them to appear patchy when dry.

Keep a piece of rag especially for this, impregnated with oil and stored in a plastic jar with a screw top. Squeeze a little oil from the oil can on to the blade and wipe over the metal and any other unpainted parts.

2 A better method of protecting tools is to use a dry wax/oil spray coating which is cleaner, easier and will not stain the surface of the work.

3 Alternatively, a soft wax can be rubbed over bare metal surfaces.

A soft wax treatment can be used to lubricate the underside or sole-plate of a bench plane to make it slide more easily, particularly through resinous woods. But again, any traces of wax left on wooden surfaces may affect the application of surface treatments or finishes.

4 As well as rusting, tools that are kept in open racks can be vulnerable to accidental damage or theft and are too easily accessible to young children. It is worth considering storing them in a strong, lockable cabinet that can be fixed to the wall or floor of your workshop.

If you are thinking of buying or making your own cabinet, make sure that it contains easily accessible storage racks. If tools are hard to reach and fiddly to replace, you simply will not bother and they will end up strewn across your workbench in a worse mess than before.

5 Tools such as chisels also present a danger to anyone handling a toolkit. It is advisable to keep them in a canvas or leather tool-roll (see page 8), both for storage in a cabinet or in a portable toolbox tray.

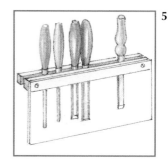

5

   If they are stored in a rack, fasten a piece of clear plastic or plywood in front of the blades to prevent anyone cutting themselves accidentally.

To avoid damaging chisel handles, only ever strike them with your hand or a mallet – never with a metal hammer.

6 Before working with any cutting-tool, check that there are no nails or other foreign bodies imbedded in the surface, as these will quickly blunt or chip metal tips.

8

7 Saw teeth can easily be protected by sliding a split plastic cover over them (the sort used to hang posters and unframed pictures will do). Alternatively, you can make your own grooved timber batten to do the same job.

Rubbing the face of a blade with candle wax or a silicone spray will help lubricate it to slide through the material you are cutting and, if applied after use, help protect the surfaces from rust.

8 Smoothing planes should always be kept in a cabinet or tool chest, with the iron either retracted or the sole-plate raised by a thin support to keep the tip of the blade clear of the shelf surface.

RESTORING RUSTY OR BROKEN TOOLS

2

A lthough most tools – including quite badly rusted ones – can be successfully restored, it may not always be worth the time and effort.

Some tools, such as worn files, obviously cannot be restored to their former glory, but can be re-shaped and ground for use as scrapers, turning tools or whatever.

Others that are badly rusted or damaged may have been weakened, making them dangerous to use. Similarly, where cutting edges have been overheated the 'temper' of the steel may well have been lost, making it incapable of holding a sharp edge for any length of time. In either case, you would be better advised to throw the tools away rather than waste time trying to restore them.

1 If a tool is just a little rusty, though, it can generally be renovated fairly easily. Light surface rust can be removed with fine wire-wool or emery paper ('wet-and-dry'). Wire-wool or a fine wire brush are also good for removing light rust from concave or recessed areas.

2 To remove heavier rust that is likely to have pitted the surface, you would be better advised to lightly sand the surface on a belt- or disc-sander. A wire brush mounted in an electric drill can be used to clean recesses, concave surfaces or heavy pitting.

When you are using power tools be careful not to overheat the cutting edge. Your aim should be to remove as little metal as possible and to keep all surfaces flat.

3 Damaged tool handles should be replaced before they break altogether in use and cause an accident. Some cheap chisels are particularly prone to this sort of defect and should be avoided.

You can remove a burr from the end of a plastic or wooden handle with a file or sandpaper.

OPPOSITE: A variety of rusted and damaged tools, some beyond restoration.

Made Simple
WOODWORKING
TOOLS

The range of woodworking tools is extremely wide and diverse, each tool being designed for a different purpose, to handle a different material or to produce a particular finish.

Their cutting edges have been designed not only to cut easily into the material but to do so without jamming or overheating. In particular, this is achieved by effectively clearing the sawdust or wood chips away as the cutting edge moves through the material.

On a saw blade, this is the reason for the shape of the teeth and the way they are set alternately from side to side. On a drill bit, the same thing is achieved by grinding the tip at an angle behind the cutting edge and by the addition of spiral flutes that allow waste to be brought to the surface.

For this reason it is extremely important when re-sharpening your tools to maintain these precise cutting and clearance angles. Otherwise the tool will not only cut less efficiently and require more effort, but may, through incorrect re-sharpening, be completely and irredeemably ruined.

BELOW: A variety of chisels and gouges.

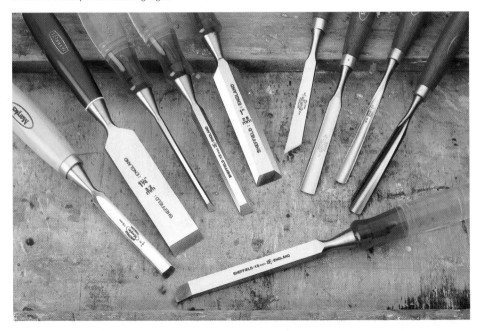

SHARPENING CHISELS

Chisels are commonly used either under hand pressure – for example when 'paring' – or driven with a mallet in heavier jobs such as cutting deep mortises.

Nowadays, with the introduction of shatterproof plastic handles, most manufacturers produce a range of chisels equally suitable for both purposes.

During manufacture, the chisel blade is first forged and then tempered to produce a steel that will hold a sharp cutting edge, before the tip angle is ground.

Initially, most manufacturers grind their chisel blades to a bevel angle of around 25°, and advise that a second bevel angle or micro-bevel of around 30° should be honed along the cutting edge.

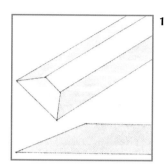

1 For general woodworking, this combination of ground and honed angles is a compromise. The aim of this is to avoid weakening the blade by making the tip too thin while maintaining good cutting characteristics.

2 A professional woodworker, on the other hand, would hone his or her chisel to a lower angle or a ground angle of 25°. This produces a much sharper cutting edge but one that is consequently weaker and needs to be treated with care to avoid chipping.

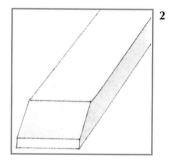

For the amateur, optimum angles of 25-30° are generally perfectly adequate, but on mortise chisels or those used for heavy chopping cuts, you may prefer a secondary honed bevel angle of 35° to give you extra strength.

SHARPENING GOUGES AND WOOD-TURNING TOOLS

With both curved gouges and also wood-turning tools, their angles should be ground before being honed.

While the external bevel can be carefully ground on a wet or dry grinding-wheel, internal bevels require a cone-shaped or rounded-edge slipstone. This can be held in a power-drill chuck, mounted in a suitable bench-stand. Again, take care to achieve a regular-angled bevel and avoid overheating the tool steel.

While care must be taken with all grinding operations, many woodturners prefer grinding their tools on a dry stone wheel for speed. Woodturning on a lathe tends to blunt tools quickly and a rapid turnaround is required.

BELOW: A variety of planes and their blades.

SHARPENING PLANES

1 Plane-blades (or irons as they are often called), are ground flat and then generally bevelled along the cutting edge to an angle of 25°, although for fine work an angle of 20° can be ground.

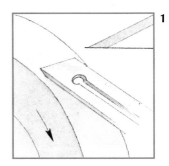

2 For smoothing- or bench-planes, a secondary micro-bevel of 30° is then honed along the cutting edge. On some special-purpose tools such as shoulder-planes, the blade is often honed to the 25° ground angle.

An angle of 25° is also sometimes adopted for block-planes and other planes used for trimming end-grain.

3 Make sure when you are sharpening spokeshave blades that the short blade is securely held – use a simple wooden holder for this purpose.

An important feature of bench smoothing planes (ie, Jack, Fore and Jointer types) is the cap-iron which is fitted to the top face of the blade. This iron must be an accurate fit against the flat blade, its leading edge mating perfectly against the surface to prevent slivers or shavings falling between the two.

If there is a gap, either the blade must be bowed (and should be replaced) or the back of the cap requires honing flat. If you have to replace the cap-iron on the blade, it should be set back approximately 1.5mm/¹₃₂in from the cutting edge for general planing. For finer cutting, reduce this distance; for coarser cutting such as roughing out, increase the distance slightly.

Spokeshave blades are ground and honed in a similar fashion to bench-plane cutters.

To ensure that you get the best performance from specialist planes such as spokeshaves, some manufacturers will include grinding and honing information with the tool when you buy it.

SHARPENING SAWS

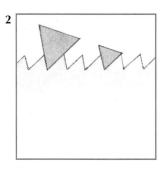

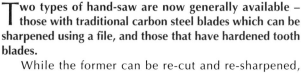

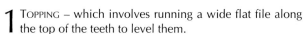

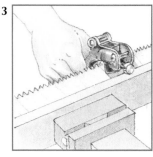

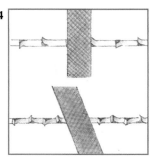

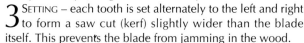

Two types of hand-saw are now generally available – those with traditional carbon steel blades which can be sharpened using a file, and those that have hardened tooth blades.

While the former can be re-cut and re-sharpened, hardened teeth cannot as the metal is extremely brittle. Although 'hardpoint' saws, as they are known, stay sharper far longer from their initial purchase, they are generally considered to be throw-away items once the sharpness has worn off.

Other types of blade, such as those used with a power jigsaw, hacksaw or pruning saw are similarly hardened and cannot be re-sharpened.

Circular saw blades are used with portable power tools and stationary saw-tables. There are two main types – carbon steel, which can be resharpened by hand, and tungsten carbide tipped, which cannot.

TCT blades are now commonly used on professional machines and are increasingly finding favour with amateurs. They have chips of tungsten carbide brazed on to their edges and then ground to a specific tooth profile. TCT blades can be ground using very specialist equipment, but need to be sent away to a professional to be re-sharpened.

There are four steps to sharpening a saw:

1 TOPPING – which involves running a wide flat file along the top of the teeth to level them.

2 SHAPING – where a tapered triangular file is used to true up the shape, height and uniformity of each tooth.

3 SETTING – each tooth is set alternately to the left and right to form a saw cut (kerf) slightly wider than the blade itself. This prevents the blade from jamming in the wood.

4 SHARPENING – on cross-cut saws, the edges of each tooth are filed to a knife edge (a micro-bevel). On rip-saws the teeth are filed square (at 90° to the face of the blade).

Major re-grinding or filing of badly-worn saw teeth is best left to an experienced saw-doctor who will have the right equipment and skill to produce regular, even teeth, set to the correct pitch.

Occasional light 'touching-up' is a job that is well within the scope of the householder and you will certainly notice the difference.

1 When you are sharpening a saw, it is necessary to hold it in a vice or bench-top jaws with a batten either side to keep the blade rigid close to the teeth.

2 Circular saw-blades should be held in a similar way between two rounded top-boards with a centre pin on which to rotate the blade.

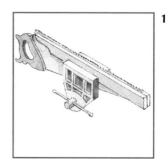

3 Never be tempted to increase the 'set', as too much of an angle will allow the saw to tip in the cut and cause it to wander off line. This allows waste material to lodge against the face of the saw, causing it to jam.

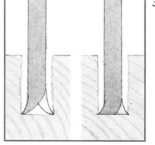

NEXT PAGE: Two panel saws and two circular saw-blades.

SHARPENING SAWS – continued

2

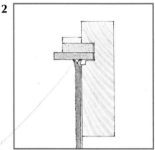

1 First, check the level of the tips of the teeth by laying the edge of a rule or steel straight edge along them. If they are excessively out of line, it will be necessary to file them flat and re-cut the teeth.

2 When you are 'topping', hold the file flat in a wooden block and run it lightly over the tips, removing metal only from the raised ones.

3 If there is only a slight difference, lightly file them down and mark any problem spots with masking tape for further attention when you come to the sharpening stage.

3

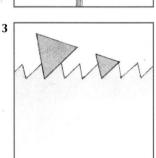

4 To correctly 'set' the saw teeth you will need a 'saw set'. The most convenient and easy-to-use sets are the pliers type, which can be adjusted to suit the size of the saw teeth (measured in terms of the number of teeth per cm/in). This size is indicated on a dial on the plier jaws.

The handles are squeezed to press the saw teeth one at a time against an anvil ground to the required angle or 'set'.

Never be tempted to increase the 'set', as too much of an angle will allow the saw to tip in the cut and cause it to wander off line. This allows waste material to lodge against the face of the saw, causing it to jam.

4

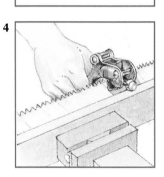

5 For 'sharpening', use a fine, 60° triangular file, preferably a good quality one that is twice as deep as the teeth you are working on.

Ensure that both file faces in contact with the V of the tooth are evenly worn and will remove equal amounts of metal each time the file is turned over.

Make light strokes to remove as little metal as possible from each edge.

6 For rip-saws (A), hold the file at right angles (90°) to the blade. For cross-cut teeth (B), hold the file at an angle of around 65°-70° to the saw blade.

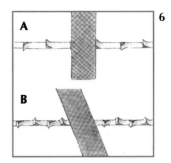

As you will be filing the edge of each alternate tooth, it is important to do the work in a logical order.

If you are right-handed you will find it easier to work with the handle of the saw on your right-hand side. Similarly, if you are left-handed you will probably find it easier to work with the handle of the saw on your left-hand side.

Start with the file on the front edge of the tooth set nearest to you so that you will also be filing the back edge of the left-hand tooth.

Move the file handle to the correct angle – square on for rip-saws, at an angle to the left for cross-cut.

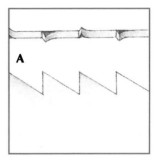

On a saw that is not too worn, you can get some feel for this from the existing bevel.

Work along one side before turning the saw around and repeating the process, filing from the handle to the right on cross-cut saws.

Aim to make the same number of filing strokes on each tooth unless one is broken or badly damaged.

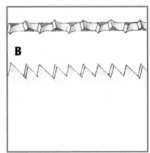

7 There are two ways you can ensure that you maintain the correct filing angle. One is to use a proprietary guide which sits over the teeth; the other is to mark the angle at regular intervals along the top edge of the clamping battens just below the teeth.

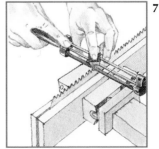

NEXT PAGE: A drill sharpening jig and a dry stone bench grinder.

SHARPENING FILES

Files are impossible to re-sharpen when they have become badly worn, but often the problem is simply that the teeth are clogged with resin, soft aluminium or similar.

To rake out this residue, you will need to use a stiff wire brush. Any remaining blockages can often be removed by rubbing the file on a piece of end-grain hardwood.

A dusting with French chalk will help prevent soft metals and other deposits adhering to the teeth.

BELOW: A well used file about to be cleaned and restored.

SHARPENING DRILL BITS

Twist drills are easy to sharpen with the aid of a jig and a dry stone grinder (see page 24).

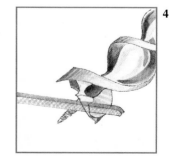

Using a jig, drill bits slot into a 'V' rest that automatically positions the tip at the required angle to the flat face of the grinding wheel. The jig can be adjusted to suit the different tip angles of the various types of bit available.

The bit is rotated through 360° against the wheel to remove an equal amount from both faces until the point is centred.

Drill sharpener attachments (see page 24) for power drills are also available and these offer an economic and efficient way to sharpen and restore twist drills for people who do not own a dry stone grinder.

1 The bit is fitted into one of four different diameter collets. The collet is then locked into its holder and fitted over the grinding wheel. Turning the collet holder from side to side grinds one side of the tip. You simply rotate the holder through 360° to grind the other. Drill tips can be lightly honed in this way or ground to remove chips from the cutting edge.

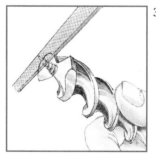

2 Auger and flat bits need to be sharpened in a different way. Here, a fine file or slipstone is required. You should aim to remove only a tiny amount of metal from the front inside face of the wings (the small upright cutting edges on the perimeter of the bit).

3 When you come to file the leading edges, take care to retain the same angle behind and keep both cutting edges level and straight.

Avoid filing the centre spur unless this is necessary.

4 Again, use a fine file and on screw-type spurs, a needle file, to clear rather than sharpen the edges of the threads.

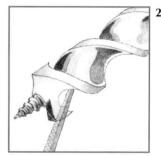

5 Flat bits can also be filed, following the original angle and ensuring that both sides are level with a flat, straight bevel.

SHARPENING ROUTER CUTTERS

Router cutters are expensive, so they are worth looking after. Those made for general woodworking are either made from high speed steel (HSS), or with tungsten carbide tips (TCT) or ground completely in tungsten carbide.

HSS cutters are suitable for use on most soft timbers but not on very hard woods or abrasive materials like chipboard. They can be honed to a far sharper edge than TCT cutters, but will need frequent attention. HSS cutters are prone to overheating in use which can ruin the temper of the steel, making it impossible to restore them.

You may also come across a type of cutter labelled HSSE. These are ground in super high speed steel and are designed for use where a particularly high quality of finish is required. They will hold their edge far better than ordinary HSS cutters.

For the more abrasive man-made materials, like chipboard and medium-density fibreboard, tungsten tipped cutters are essential to avoid burning both the cutter and the wood.

Tungsten carbide is a very hard material, but it is also brittle, so TCT cutters must be handled and stored with care. They are significantly more expensive than HSS cutters, but should last up to 10 times longer.

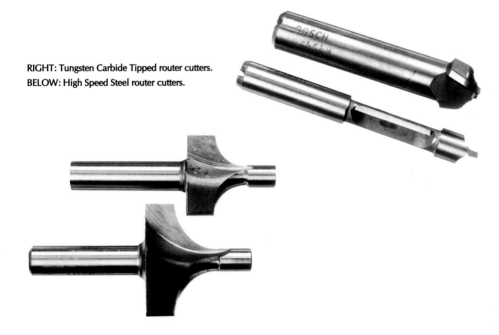

RIGHT: Tungsten Carbide Tipped router cutters.
BELOW: High Speed Steel router cutters.

1 Router cutters are shaped to produce flutes, radial relief and clearance angles. It is extremely important to maintain these when sharpening the cutters.

HSS cutters can be honed using a good quality oilstone.

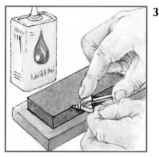

2 Prior to honing, you must remove all ball-bearing guides. Scrape the cutter clean and then use a solvent and wire brush or wire wool to remove any resin build-up.

3 Place the flute of the cutter on to the corner of the stone and draw the cutter up and down the stone until a burr is produced on the edge.

4 The burr should be removed with a fine slipstone without changing the cutter edge profile.

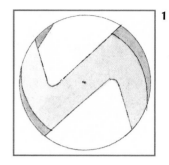

Never attempt to sharpen a cutter on its outside edge as this will affect clearance angles and the shape of the cutter. If a cutter is slightly chipped, no amount of honing will repair this; send it back to the manufacturer or a saw doctor for re-grinding. Badly-chipped cutters cannot be repaired and will have to replaced.

5 TCT cutters can be honed the same way as HSS cutters, but a diamond particle abrasive is needed rather than an oilstone.

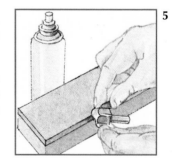

There are different types of diamond abrasive. With one a diamond slurry is sprayed over a tile; with another, the diamonds are embedded into the face of an aluminium base.

NEXT PAGE: A selection of garden tools which need to be kept sharp to be safe and efficient.

GARDEN AND HOUSEHOLD TOOLS

The cutting edges of most garden tools do not need to be sharpened to the same degree of accuracy as those used in the workshop.

That is not to say they do not need to be sharp, but generally grinding with a fine grade stone is sufficient to keep them working well. Exceptions to this rule are secateurs and pruning shears which need to be sharpened accurately to cut through sturdy plant stems.

SHARPENING AXES

Axes should be ground on a whetstone to ensure that the temper of their steel is not lost. If you do not have a whetstone, a belt- or disc-sander can be used, but take care not to overheat the metal.

If you require a very fine finish, this can be honed with a handstone. This is a round stone with a grooved edge which allows the fingers to grip it clear of the blade. Handstones are also useful for honing other chopping and digging tools. They are made from silicone carbide and can be lubricated with oil or water.

SHARPENING SHEARS, SECATEURS AND LOPPERS

The edge bevel on grass shear blades can be sharpened with a flat scythe stone, following the original bevel angle on the outer edges only. Use water as a lubricant.

Lightly stroke the inside face to remove any burrs, keeping the stone flat on the blade. If you are working on a bench grindstone, use a tool-rest to hold the shears at the required angle and part the two blades before running them separately against the wheel. De-burr the opposite face on a flat oil- or waterstone before re-assembling the shears.

Secateurs and loppers should be honed carefully using a slipstone around the concave bevel. The opposing square edge against which it closes should not need to be trued up unless the edge has been damaged or burred by accidentally cutting into thick wire or other hard material.

Pruning cutters and loppers can be sharpened in similar fashion, using a flat or rounded hand oilstone or slipstone.

With all tools that have a scissor action, you must ensure that the mating faces are perfectly flat and that the pivot is tight enough to keep the cutting edges against each other.

SHARPENING CHAINSAWS

Both chisel- and chipper-type chainsaw teeth should be regularly sharpened to minimise the risk of the chain jamming and snatching when you are cutting wood with it.

Hand-sharpening can be performed using a hardened, round chainsaw file. These are available in various diameters to match the range of tooth sizes, but should be handled with care. It is essential to maintain the correct sharpening angle and retain the tooth profile.

In most cases the chain can be sharpened without removing it from the bar. Take a minimal amount of metal from each tooth with a few light strokes, working in the gullet of the tooth only. Do not remove metal from the top of the tooth.

Sharpening guides for use with chainsaw files are readily available from garden centres and other garden tool stores. These simply fit over the chain and edge of the bar to keep the file at the correct angle.

If, after light sharpening, a chain still does not cut easily, return the complete saw to a specialist for attention rather than risk ruining the blade and injuring the operator.

After sharpening the chain, take the opportunity to check over the remainder of the saw, making sure that all parts are securely fitted and all the safety features are in working order.

In particular, it is worth checking that the chain oiler is clear and that the chain is correctly tensioned.

BELOW: A chainsaw with a chainsaw sharpening guide.

SHARPENING SCYTHES

Scythes, sickles and other curved blades can all be honed using a scythe stone.

1 Either round tapered, flat ground or oval in section, these are held in the palm of the hand and rubbed along the edge of the blade, working from the handle out.

Take care that the stone remains flat against the blade at all times, otherwise a rounded edge will form. Lubricate with oil or water.

Scythe stones are also handy for truing and honing the edges of spades, hoes and trenching tools.

Made Simple
SHARPENING
EQUIPMENT

Sharpening tools is a skill that needs to be learned and practise is required if you want to become fast and proficient. It is important to recognise your limitations initially and work slowly to avoid damaging either yourself or your tools.

BELOW: A bench grinder and safety equipment.

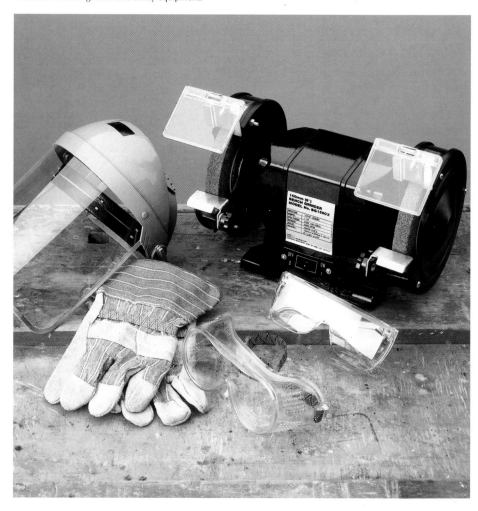

Made Simple

GRINDERS AND GRINDING

Grinding metal on a drystone, abrasive disc or belt inevitably throws hot particles up into the air. It is essential to wear safety glasses or goggles to protect your eyes or a visor that will give you full-face protection.

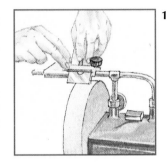

1 Always use a tool rest, clamp or holder to support the blade you are working on. These are built-in on many drystone grinders. On cheaper models they consist of bent steel brackets which are fine for general grinding but less satisfactory for sharpening work.

It is worth considering buying and fitting a better tool-rest if you cannot afford to buy a more expensive grinder from the outset which will have a range of jigs and better quality rests built-in.

2 To protect your hands from burns, it is always sensible to wear gloves when you are working with a grinder.

3 It essential too, to ensure that any combustible material is kept well away from the sparks.

4 All drystone grinders should be fitted with adequate spark/eye guards by their manufacturer, but all too often these are not used because they 'get in the way' or break and are not replaced.

Safety is paramount when you are working with power tools – do not be tempted to cut corners.

WHICH GRINDER?

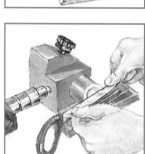

Cutting edge tools are generally ground 'dry' on either a high-speed bench grinder or abrasive belt, or 'wet' on a slow grinding-wheel running in a water- or oil-bath.

Both horizontal- and vertical-mounted grinding wheels and stones are available, grinding being carried out on the perimeter edge of the latter to produce a concave or hollow ground face on the tool, or flat against the side face of the former.

It comes down to personal preference when deciding what type of grinder to buy. Flat-face grinding will produce a very smooth polished bevel that requires minimal honing if the wheel is of a high grade, whereas the hollow bevel produced by grinding against the perimeter of a wheel requires honing to establish a smooth flat micro bevel.

Generally-speaking, the larger the diameter of the wheel the better, as this reduces the hollowing effect. If the hollow is too exaggerated, the bevel face can be ground too thin and become weakened.

For general woodworking tools, a 200mm/8in minimum wheel diameter is recommended, but at this size there is little allowance for wear and re-dressing.

Beginners will find it easier to hone a hollow ground bevel, as this involves removing a tiny amount of metal from the tip of the tool and the hollow does provide some clearance behind the cutting edge.

1 Bench grinders with integral motors are the most convenient and tend to be more efficient.

2 Some smaller units can be purchased as accessories to be driven by an electric drill.

Both 'dry' and 'wet' stones are available, although most units of this type are fitted with small-diameter grinding wheels. Where they come into their own is for occasional sharpening jobs and they are often supplied with alternative grade stones for grinding both carbon steel tools and carbide-tipped tools such as masonry drills.

With small grinders of this type, it is more sensible to buy replacement stones rather than to bother re-facing them when they become worn.

HOW TO GRIND CUTTING EDGES

When you are grinding against a wheel, the tool or blade can be run either with or against the rotation of the stone. The actual difference in terms of the sharpness of the cutting edge will be minimal but there are other factors to consider when deciding which way to grind.

When you grind against the rotation, the edge automatically presses into the stone, increasing the pressure between the grinding faces.

This certainly speeds up the grinding process and tends to expose the abrasive, preventing it from clogging too quickly. However, this technique also increases the risk of the blade edge digging into the stone and jamming.

Whether you are in the habit of digging into the stone or not, all grinding wheels and stones require regular dressing with a suitable wheel-dresser to keep the grinding faces flat and true.

To sharpen an edge on either a dry or wet stone, you should aim to move the blade back and forth across the face of the stone, maintaining the bevel angle against the tool-rest and keeping the edge of the blade square to the face.

Check the condition of the ground face regularly to ensure that only sufficient metal is being removed to expose an even, clean surface. Take care to lay the ground face back against the wheel at the same angle as before when you replace it.

With curved gouges and wood-turning tools, roll the rounded face of the tool against the face of the wheel, ensuring that the bevel angle remains the same on both edges.

Having ground the face, remove the edge burr by laying the rear face of the blade flat on an oilstone and drawing it across the surface. Do not raise the blade from the face of the stone or you will produce an unwanted bevel.

RIGHT: A medium and a small sized grinding wheel.

DRYSTONE GRINDING

Drystone bench grinders are best-suited to grinding hardened metal cutting tools or metal components. They are readily available to amateur woodworkers and home improvers and can be used for general-purpose grinding as well as tool-sharpening.

Drystone grinders run at high speeds – typically around 30,000 rpm – which makes them ideal for sharpening woodworking tools such as gouges and scrapers which lose their edge relatively quickly. At that sort of speed, it only takes a few minutes to restore the edge and get back to work.

The drawback, of course, is that a lot of frictional heat can build up in those few seconds, and care must be taken not to 'draw' the temper of the tool steel and ruin the tool.

To reduce the risk of overheating, the tool will need to be regularly quenched in water to cool it during sharpening. But even then it will be difficult to prevent the thin tip of the cutting edge from overheating. For this reason, the sharpness of the edge is unlikely to be as durable as that of a tool ground on a slow whetstone.

If you do overheat the tip by accident, you will need to grind the metal well back to a point not affected by the loss of temper. Hardened and stainless steels should also be quenched during sharpening, though they are less vulnerable than carbon steels.

Generally, grinding wheels are made of corundum or more commonly aluminium oxide and are available in grades from coarse (around 36 grit) to fine (80 grit). Cheap grinding wheels tend to wear quickly and unevenly, leaving the face of the tool uneven.

Most dry bench-grinders are double-ended to carry both a fine and coarse wheel or to take wire brushes or a tapered spindle for fitting polishing pads and mops.

LEFT: When quenching the tool, place as much of the blade length as you can into the coolant to draw the heat from along its length and not just from the tip. Otherwise the heat from further up the blade will quickly transfer back down to the tip when you re-commence the sharpening process.

WHETSTONE GRINDING

1

The basic differences between dry and whetstone grinding are the speed at which the stone revolves and the fact that with the latter, water is continuously carried over the face of the stone to cool both stone and tool.

This makes for a lot slower grinding action but virtually eliminates the risk of overheating the tool steel. Whetstone grinders tend to run at between 50 and 150 rpm.

Each grinder incorporates a reduction drive mechanism to control the speed, which adds considerably to the cost. On large-diameter stones, the speed is often reduced still further to prevent the water being sprayed around.

Horizontal stones can be run at faster speeds – nearer 400-500 rpm, the centrifugal effect helping to spread the coolant evenly across the face of the stone. This coolant also serves to wash waste particles away. Horizontal whetstones produce a faster grinding action than vertical ones.

Whetstone grinding wheels were originally made from natural sandstone, but these days more often consist of man-made ceramics that contain an aluminium oxide abrasive.

While man-made stones tend to grind faster and are more durable, natural ones are still regarded as superior when it comes to producing very fine or polished finishes.

1 While safety glasses should be worn and combustible materials cleared away, accidents are far less likely to occur with a whetstone than a drystone. Sparks are rarely produced and the chances of particles flying off the stone are far less.

The water trough or container on all whetstone grinders should be removable to allow for regular cleaning to prevent waste particles from coagulating into a solid mass.

WORKING WITH OILSTONES

Honing is usually done on an oilstone. Oilstones can be made of natural stone, reconstituted stone or man-made materials such as aluminium oxide.

Natural stones tend to be more expensive and wear quicker. They are favoured by craftsmen and wood carvers who require very fine edges.

Whichever type you go for, it is important that it is hard enough to maintain a flat surface. Cheap stones soon hollow, resulting in rounded and uneven cutting edges.

Even the best quality stones will wear in time, of course, but they can be successfully restored over and over again. This is done by rubbing the face on a flat slab of marble, plate glass or even a paving slab, using water and silver sand as a grinding compound. Carborundum powder can be used in place of silver sand and is particularly effective on the harder, artificial stones.

The use of oil on the face during honing not only lubricates the surface but helps to prevent particles of metal clogging the pores of the stone and 'glazing' its surface.

If you have a stone that has become clogged in this way, try soaking it in petrol and then brushing it with a stiff brush that has also been soaked in the petrol.

Oilstones are generally available in three grades – fine, medium and coarse. For most purposes, medium and fine grades are suitable and can be bought together on a single, double-faced stone.

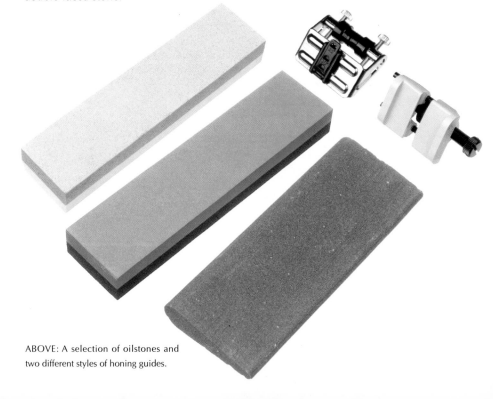

ABOVE: A selection of oilstones and two different styles of honing guides.

1 Before starting each honing session, fill the pores of the stone with oil. To do this, lay the stone in an oil bath, turning it over so that both faces are soaked. A bath need consist of no more than a piece of plastic with its edges raised to prevent the oil escaping. However, many better quality stones – India stones for example – are pre-soaked in the factory and do not require this treatment.

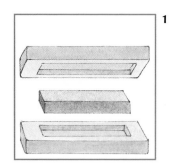

A box made from two off-cuts of wood are an excellent solution for permanent storage – preventing the stone from being damaged – and for occasional oiling.

2 Secure the stone either in a wooden box or on a wooden block, that can be secured in a vice or hooked over the side of a work bench.

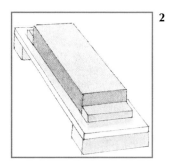

3 Before running a cutting edge over any stone, apply a thin layer of oil across the surface to keep the particles of debris floating.

4 It is often suggested that the blade being sharpened should be moved in a figure-of-eight pattern so that you are working over the entire face of the stone and keeping wear in any one spot to a minimum.

However, for the inexperienced amateur this is a tall order since the cutting edge can easily be rounded off during this circular movement.

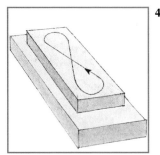

It is quite possible to work in straight lines up and down the stone without causing excessive wear and this is probably a safer option to begin with.

A honing guide is a blade-holder fitted with a wide steel roller or wheel that can be run over the surface of the stone. The guide automatically sets and maintains the correct bevel angle for you.

5 Having honed the face bevel to the required angle, turn the blade over and wipe it flat across the stone to remove the fine burr that will have formed along the cutting edge.

6 Always wipe dirty oil from the face of the stone with a lint-free cloth when you have finished a honing session.

TOOL RESTS

1: It is important that your grinder is fitted with a tool-rest to support the blade at a set angle.
2: To handle wide blades, a sliding tool-rest is needed so that the full width can be run across the face of the stone.

HOW TO HONE CUTTING EDGES

1: Cutting-edge tools need to be kept sharp by regular honing on an oil or water-lubricated stone. Honing removes any grinding marks on the tip and produces a sharp, polished edge that will slice far more easily into or through the material being worked.
2: With single-bevel angles, the whole face of the bevel can be lightly honed. With a double bevel, only the tip angle needs to be sharpened.
3: If you are careful, you can in theory go on honing single bevels almost indefinitely, though some variation in the bevel angle will almost certainly creep in or an edge get chipped, forcing you to re-grind the blade eventually.
4: With double bevels, you will find that after only a few honing sessions, a wide bevel is beginning to form along the cutting edge and this will then have to be re-ground to restore the original angle.

WORKING WITH SLIPSTONES

1: Tools like gouges that have a curved blade cannot be sharpened on a flat surface like that of a conventional oilstone. For this type of job you need a slipstone.
2: Slipstones are small, hand-held oilstones that are specifically shaped for honing awkward, narrow or internal curved surfaces.
3: Like a conventional oilstone, a slipstone will need to be lubricated before you can use it and for this reason make a holder from scrap wood for each one you buy.

WORKING WITH DIAMOND WHETSTONES

1: Diamond is one of the hardest materials known to man, which makes it ideal for honing anything from carbon steel to tungsten carbide.
2: Diamond whetstones are a relatively new development and are far from cheap, but once purchased they will last almost indefinitely.
3: The industrial grade diamonds used are set in nickel and mounted on a perforated steel plate that is injection-moulded on a base made from glass fibre and polycarbonate.
4: Diamond whetstones are colour-coded according to their grit rating.
5: Water is used as a lubricant, but only a very light pressure and relatively few strokes are needed to produce a very sharp edge.

Photography props supplied by:

Nina Barough Styling

As credited, photographic material reproduced by kind permission of:

Elizabeth Whiting Associates